MARY ROBINSON

A President in Progress

FORMER PRESIDENTS OF IRELAND

Douglas Hyde 1938–1945

Seán T. Ó Ceallaigh 1945–1959

Éamon de Valera 1959–1973

Erskine Childers 1973–1974

Cearbhaill O'Dalaigh 1974–1976

Patrick J. Hillery 1976–1990

BUNREACHT NA hÉIREANN
(CONSTITUTION OF IRELAND)

Article 12

1. There shall be a President of Ireland (Uachtarán na hÉireann), hereinafter called the President, who shall take precedence over all other persons in the State and who shall exercise and perform the powers and functions conferred on the President by this Constitution and by law.

1 July 1937

MARY ROBINSON

A President in Progress

TEXT BY DEIRDRE MCQUILLAN

GILL & MACMILLAN

Gill & Macmillan Ltd
Goldenbridge
Dublin 8
with associated companies throughout the world
© Text Deirdre McQuillan 1994
0 7171 2251 4

Picture Research: Adrienne Murphy
and Monica McInerney

Design and print origination by
Identikit Design Consultants, Dublin

Colour Separations by Ultragraphics Ltd

Printed by ColourBooks Ltd, Dublin

A catalogue record is available for this book
from the British Library.

1   3   5   4   2

INTRODUCTION

August 1990 Mary Robinson, presidential candidate, is given a helping hand on Inishmore, Aran Islands.

On Monday 3 December 1990 at the age of 46, Mary Teresa Winifred Robinson née Bourke, of Ballina, Co. Mayo, was inaugurated seventh President of Ireland, following the first presidential election

years. A

lawyer, former politician, wife and mother of three children, she became the first woman to hold the highest office in the land and the youngest. By general agreement, it was an extraordinary victory.

ech marked by both d celebration, she

pledged to represent 'a new Ireland, open, tolerant, inclusive' and concluded with the words of a poet, 'I am of Ireland ... come dance with me in Ireland.' Thus began the most spectacular presidency in the history of the state.

As she completes the fourth of her seven-year term of office, Mary Robinson has set precedents and fulfilled promises. She has transformed with great style and vigour what had been perceived as a largely ceremonial job, in ways no one would have envisaged or thought possible, investing it with a new dynamism and relevance. Her presidency is not only active and hardworking, but also one distinguished by imagination, vision and commitment.

She has visited towns and villages in Ireland no President has ever visited before, has opened up her residence, Áras an Uachtaráin, to the people of Ireland north and south, and has travelled extensively overseas. She has carried out more than two thousand public engagements and endorsed the work of many small groups as well as supporting major organisations and projects.

Abroad she has been bestowed with many awards for her human rights record, and is recognised internationally as representing a new image of Ireland. The *New York Times* described her as one of the most remarkable heads of state in the world today despite her lack of executive power. By sheer force of character, she has achieved a popular moral leadership, their writer concluded.

This book is a visual record of these first years in office as she moves into the second half of her presidency. Taking her inaugural address as its starting point, it has been divided into chapters, each reflecting the themes of her presidency and showing how she has developed and honoured her undertakings.

No doubt there will be more surprises in the years ahead, but few would deny that she has become, as she promised, a president for *all* the people, borne out by a popularity rating of ninety-three per cent, from a poll taken in June 1993. In the words of one Fianna Fáil politician quoted in *The Irish Times* after her trip to Australia, 'she's like Ayers Rock ... a phenomenon. All you can do is walk around her.'

Inaugural Speech

Address by Mary Robinson on the occasion of her inauguration
as President of Ireland, 3 December 1990

Citizens of Ireland, mná na hÉireann agus fir na hÉireann, you have chosen me to represent you and I am humbled by and grateful for your trust.

The Ireland I will be representing is a new Ireland, open, tolerant, inclusive. Many of you who voted for me did so without sharing all of my views. This, I believe, is a significant signal of change, a sign, however modest, that we have already passed the threshold to a new pluralist Ireland.

The recent revival of an old concept of the fifth province expresses this emerging Ireland of tolerance and empathy. The old Irish term for province is *coiceað*, meaning a 'fifth'; and yet as everyone knows, there are only four geographical provinces on this island. So where is the fifth? The fifth province is not anywhere here or there, north or south, east or west. It is a place within each one of us – that place that is open to the other, that swinging door which allows us to venture out and others to venture in. Ancient legends divided Ireland into four quarters and a 'middle', although they differed about the location of this middle or fifth province. While Tara was the political centre of Ireland, tradition has it that this fifth province acted as a second centre, a necessary balance. If I am a symbol of anything I would like to be a symbol of this reconciling and healing fifth province.

My primary role as President will be to represent this state. But the state is not the only model of community with which Irish people can and do identify. Beyond our state there is a vast community of Irish emigrants extending not only across our neighbouring island – which has provided a home away from home for several Irish generations – but also throughout the continents of North America, Australia and of course Europe itself. There are over 70 million people living on this globe who claim Irish descent. I will be proud to represent them. And I would like to see Áras an Uachtaráin serve – on something of an annual basis – as a place where our emigrant communities could send representatives for a get together of the extended Irish family abroad.

There is yet another level of community which I will represent. Not just the national, not just the global, but the local community. Within our state there are growing numbers of local and regional communities determined to express their own creativity, identity, heritage and initiative in new and exciting ways. In my travels throughout Ireland I have found local community groups thriving on a new sense of self-confidence and self-empowerment. Whether it was groups concerned with adult education, employment initiative, women's support, local history and heritage, environmental concern or community culture, one of the most enriching discoveries was to witness the extent of this local empowerment at work.

As President I will seek to the best of my abilities to promote this growing sense of local participatory democracy, this energising movement of self-development and self-expression which is surfacing more and more at grassroots level. This is the face of modern Ireland.

Ba mhaith liom a rá go bhfuair mé taitneamh agus pléisiúr as an taisteal a rinne mé le míosa anuas ar fuaid na hÉireann. Is fíor álainn agus iontach an tír atá againn, agus is álainn an pobal iad muintir na hÉireann.

Fuair mé teachtaireacht ón bpobal seo agus mé ag dul timpeall: 'Teastaíonn Uachtarán uainn gur féidir linn bheith bródúil aisti, ach níos mó ná sin, gur féidir linn bheith bródúil lena chéile – toisce gcur Éireannaigh sinn, agus go bhfuil traidisiúin agus cultúr álainn againn.'

Is cuid án tábhactach don gcultúr sin an Ghaeilge – an teanga bheo – fé mar atá á labhairt sa Ghaeltacht agus ag daoine eile ar fuaid na hÉireann.

Tá aistear eile le déanamh anois agam – aistear cultúrtha, leis an saibhreas iontach atá sa teanga Ghaeilge a bhaint amach díom féin.

Tá súil agam go leanfaidh daoine eile mé atá ar mo nós fhéin – beagán as cleatach sa Ghaeilge – agus go raghaimíd ar aghaidh le chéile le taithneamh agus pléisiúr a fháil as ár dteanga álainn féinn.

TRANSLATION:

[I want to say how much I enjoyed travelling around Ireland over the last few months. Ours is a truly beautiful country and the Irish people are a wonderful race.

I got a message from the people that they wanted a President they could be proud of, but more than that, that we could take pride together – in our Irishness and our wonderful heritage and culture.

The Irish language is an important part of that culture, as spoken in the Gaeltacht areas and around the country. I am about to embark on another journey – a cultural voyage of discovery of the wealth and beauty of the Irish language. I hope others who, like myself, are somewhat out of practice, will join me on this journey, and that we will progress together to enjoy to the full our own beautiful language.]

The best way we can contribute to a new integrated Europe of the 1990s is by having a confident sense of our Irishness. Here again we must play to our strengths – take full advantage of our vibrant cultural resources in music, art, drama, literature and film; value the role of our educators; promote and preserve our unique environment and geographical resources of relatively pollution-free lakes, rivers,

landscapes and seas; encourage and publicly support local initiative projects in aquaculture, forestry, fishing, alternative energy and small scale technology.

Looking outwards from Ireland, I would like on your behalf to contribute to the international protection and promotion of human rights. One of our greatest national resources has always been, and still is, our ability to serve as a moral and political conscience in world affairs. We have a long history of providing spiritual, cultural and social assistance to other countries in need – most notably in Latin America, Africa and other Third World countries. And we can continue to promote these values by taking principled and independent stands on issues of international importance.

As the elected President of this small democratic country I assume office at a vital moment in Europe's history. Ideological boundaries that have separated East and West are withering away at an astounding pace. Eastern countries are seeking to participate as full partners in a restructured and economically buoyant Europe. The stage is set for a new common Europe based on respect for human rights, pluralism, tolerance and openness to new ideas. The European Convention on Human

Rights – one of the main achievements of the Council of Europe – is asserting itself as the natural Constitution for the new Europe. These developments have created one of the major challenges for the 1990s.

If it is time, as Joyce's Stephen Dedalus remarked, that the Irish began to forge in the smithy of our souls 'the uncreated conscience of our race' – might we not also take on the still 'uncreated conscience' of the wider international community? Is it not time that the small started believing again that it is beautiful, that the periphery can rise up and speak out on equal terms with the centre, that the most outlying island community of the European Community really has something 'strange and precious' to contribute to the sea-change presently sweeping through the entire continent of Europe? As a native of Ballina, one of the most western towns in the most western province of the most western nation in Europe, I want to say – 'the West's awake'.

I turn to another place close to my heart, Northern Ireland. As the elected choice of the people of this part of our island I want to extend the hand of friendship and of love to both communities in the other part. And I want to do this with no strings attached, no hidden agenda. As the

person chosen by you to symbolise this Republic and to project our self-image to others, I will seek to encourage mutual understanding and tolerance between all the different communities sharing this island.

In seeking to do this I shall rely to a large extent on symbols. But symbols are what unite and divide people. Symbols give us our identity, our self-image, our way of explaining ourselves to ourselves and to others. Symbols in turn determine the kinds of stories we tell; and the stories we tell determine the kind of history we make and remake. I want Áras an Uachtaráin to be a place where people can tell diverse stories – in the knowledge that there is someone there to listen.

I want this presidency to promote the telling of stories – stories of celebration through the arts and stories of conscience and of social justice. As a woman, I want women who have felt themselves outside history to be written back into history, in the words of Eavan Boland, 'finding a voice where they found a vision'.

May God direct me so that my presidency is one of justice, peace and love. May I have the fortune to preside over an Ireland at a time of exciting transformation when we enter a new Europe where old wounds can be healed, a time when, in the words of Seamus Heaney, 'hope and history rhyme'. May it be a presidency where I the President can sing to you, citizens of Ireland, the joyous refrain of the 14th century Irish poet as recalled by W.B. Yeats: 'I am of Ireland ... come dance with me in Ireland.'

Go raibh míle maith agaibh go léir.

St Patrick's Hall in Dublin Castle where the inauguration began with an interdenominational prayer service. Over 500 people were in attendance including An Taoiseach Mr Charles J. Haughey, members of the Government and Council of State, as well as personal guests.

VICTORY AND VALEDICTION

On 9 November 1990 after one of the most extraordinary and eventful elections in Irish politics, Mary Robinson was declared President of Ireland, winning by a margin of 86,557 votes. Exactly six months earlier she had begun her presidential campaign in the tiny village of Allihies in south west Cork. A journey of 'joy and discovery' as she put it on the campaign trail, ended in a triumphant and impressive victory. This victory was also a valediction, she said, a farewell to those who had worked so hard on her campaign.

Her inauguration as the seventh President of Ireland took place with great fanfare and ceremony and international news coverage on Monday 3 December 1990 in Dublin Castle.

November 1990 Moment of victory:
A triumphant Mary Robinson is
cheered by jubilant supporters at the Royal
Dublin Society after the election count. On the
left is Aoife Breslin of Labour Youth.

■ Victor and vanquished: flanked on the
right by the defeated candidate Brian Lenihan,
Fianna Fáil's presidential nominee and on the
left by Labour leader Dick Spring and An
Taoiseach Mr Charles J. Haughey, Mary
Robinson declares, 'I will be a President for all
the people.' She also paid tribute to the people
of Ireland who had voted for her and
concluded, 'I don't know whether to dance or
to sing — and I have done both.'

■ Newly decorated and refurbished, St
Patrick's Hall in Dublin Castle, hung with
chandeliers and the banners of the Irish
knights on the morning of the inauguration.

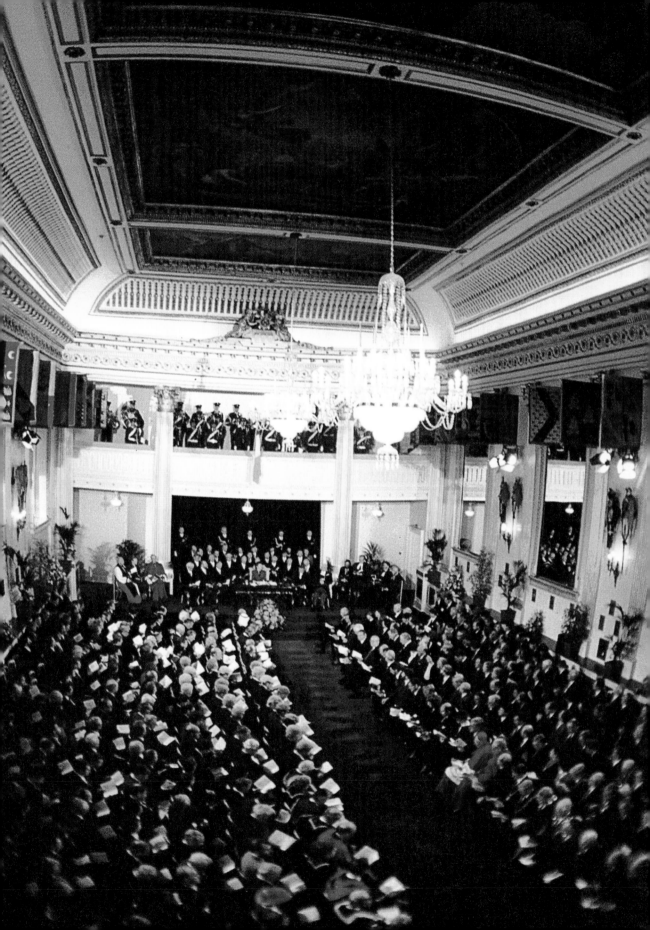

Mary Robinson and her husband Nick leave their Sandford Road home in Ranelagh for Dublin Castle on inauguration day. The President was wearing a purple silk moiré jacket by Louise Kennedy and a short black skirt. The gold necklace and earrings were a gift to her from the Robinson family.

■ Nick Robinson by his wife's side after her inauguration.

rchbishop Cathal Daly of Armagh shares a few words with Dr Robin Eames, Primate of All Ireland at the prayer service in St Patrick's Hall.

■ The Chief Justice Mr Justice Thomas Finlay administers the Declaration of Office of the President and the oath in which the new President promises to maintain the Constitution and uphold the law. The ceremony was followed by a 21-gun salute and trumpet fanfare. 'My eyes kept filling with tears,' recalled former Minister for Education, Gemma Hussey, describing the emotion of the occasion.

P resident Mary Robinson with An Taoiseach Charles J. Haughey; Attorney General Mr John Murray; former President Patrick Hillery; former Taoiseach Liam Cosgrave; Bobby Molloy; Bertie Ahern; Desmond O'Malley; Cathaoirleach of the Senate Seán Doherty; Minister for Foreign Affairs Gerard Collins; Nick Robinson; Mary O'Rourke; Mr Justice Liam Hamilton; Provost of TCD Dr A.J. McConnell and former Minister for Education Padraig Faulkner.

■ The inaugural address: 'May God direct me so that my presidency is one of justice, peace and love....'

Presudent Robinson, Supreme Commander of the Defence Forces, accompanied by officer-in-charge Captain Tom Boyce and her aide-de-camp Colonel Patrick McNally, inspecting the Guard of Honour drawn from the Second Infantry Battalion, Cathal Brugha Barracks after her inauguration.

■ Leaving Dublin Castle with husband Nick, Tánaiste John Wilson and Minister for Foreign Affairs Gerard Collins.

The presidential motorcade making its way up O'Connell Street.

■ Led by thirty-six presidential blue motorcycles driven by members of the Second Cavalry Squadron, Cathal Brugha Barracks, the presidential motorcade arrives in the Phoenix Park en route to Áras an Uachtaráin.

The President arriving at her new residence for a celebratory lunch for over sixty guests. These included members of the Bourke and Robinson families; Eavan Boland, poet; Rita Childers, widow of President Erskine Childers; Leonard Davies, Chef de Cabinet of the Council of Europe; Frances Fitzgerald, chairwoman, Council for the Status of Women; Maurice Hayes, Ombudsman for Northern Ireland; Seamus Heaney, poet; Catherine Lalumiere, Secretary General of the Council of Europe; Anthony Lester Q.C., chairman Interrights, London; Rev Professor Enda McDonagh, Professor of Moral Theology, St Patrick's College, Maynooth; Edward McParland FTCD, architectural historian; Michael O'Boyle, legal adviser at the Court of Human Rights, Strasbourg; Bride Rosney, special adviser to Ms Robinson; John Temple Lang, director, Directorate for Competition, European Community; John Alderdice, Alliance Party leader; Dr Maeve Hillery, wife of the former President Dr Patrick Hillery; John Hume, SDLP leader; Ken Maginnis, Ulster Unionist Party; Gearoid O Maolmhichil, National Youth Council; Dick Spring, Labour Party.

■ The official photograph of the new President as she took up office.

ÁRAS AN

UACHTARÁIN

Á ras an Uachtaráin (literally the house of the President) in the Phoenix Park became the residence of the first President of Ireland in 1938. Formerly the Vice-Regal lodge and handed over after independence in 1922, this palatial white building, set in 160 acres of parkland, started life in 1751 as a modest brick house. It was built by Nathaniel Clements, ranger of the park, who amassed a considerable fortune during the development of Georgian Dublin.

In 1782 it was purchased as an 'occasional residence' for the Lord Lieutenant and extensively enlarged to include the handsome Ionic portico on the garden front, which can be seen through the gap in the trees from the main road through the park.

Inside, one of the finest plaster ceilings in Ireland was installed in the reception room in the 1940s. It represents 'Jupiter and the Elements' and was brought from Mespil House, Dublin which was then being demolished for flats. In the 1950s casts of the famous wall panels from Riverstown House in Cork by the distinguished stuccodores, the Francini brothers, were erected in both the State drawing room and in a newly constructed gallery. These plaster transcripts of an allegorical painting by Poussin — now in the Louvre — represent 'Time Rescuing Truth from the Assault of Discord and Envy'. Carpets for the main reception rooms and gallery area — designed and made by Donegal Carpets in Killybegs — were also installed around this time.

President Robinson is the first President of Ireland to break with tradition by choosing to live above the State Rooms rather than in the west wing. She has also promised to carry out further renovations and improvements to enhance the building and make it more accessible. The basement area is being converted into a Visitors' Centre which will tell the story of the house and is due to open in 1995.

September 1992 President Robinson being greeted by an autistic youth from James Connolly House at the start of 'The Great Day', the Dublin taxi drivers' annual outing for children with disabilities, at Parnell Square, Dublin.

A President
for All the People

In terms of the active, working presidency promised by Mary Robinson during her election campaign, her performance to date has been impressive by any standards. At the end of her first twelve months in office, she had fulfilled more than 800 engagements, written more than 700 speeches, attended dozens of sporting events and made five trips abroad. She has met, literally, tens of thousands of people.

While her schedule now takes in more overseas travel, at home she undertakes approximately four or five appointments a day. Her husband Nick once paid tribute to her remarkable stamina by saying that she has the constitution of an ox.

Travelling to all corners of Ireland and encouraging contact, President Robinson continues to fulfil her policy of visiting all counties every year. She has visited prisoners and pensioners, has attended the funeral of a homeless man and the funeral of a king. She has opened up Áras an Uachtaráin to the people of Ireland, north and south, has welcomed dignitaries of church and state as well as more marginalised groups like the travellers, the unemployed, gays and lesbians. As Supreme Commander of the Defence Forces, she was the first President in office ever to visit an army base, when she visited the Curragh in November 1993. She has inaugurated special family days, senior citizens days, and many other events in the grounds of her Phoenix Park residence. Each December she hosts a party for around 400 returned Irish development workers. The list of her firsts is now incalculable.

Most importantly, as a President of the people, she has affirmed her belief in the importance of local and regional communities around the country, 'determined to express their own creativity, identity, heritage and initiative in new and exciting ways'. This grassroots movement of self-development is, she believes, the face of modern Ireland.

Her visits have not only psychological but practical side effects too: the one to the Women's Aid refuge in Dublin resulted in a complete £10,000 refurbishment of the premises and when she accepted an invitation to open a Women's Studies Centre in Galway, a new bungalow was promised to house it. According to one presidential aide, 'You get used to the smell of fresh paint when you travel with the President.'

February 1993 President Robinson officially launches ICON, the Inner City Organisations Network at the Fire Station Artists' Studio in Buckingham Street.

■ August 1993 President Robinson with Anthony McDonnell of Dublin, a HIV positive patient at St James Hospital, Dublin where she officially opened a newly refurbished unit for AIDS patients.

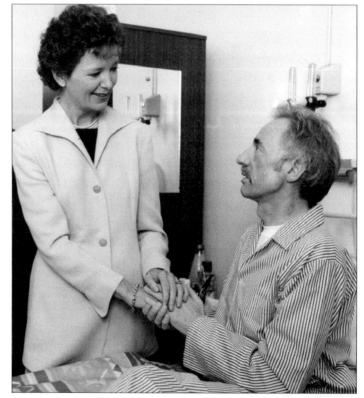

February 1994 Launching Brian Nolan and Tim Callan's book *Poverty and Policy in Ireland*, President Robinson said that 'one of the achievements of our society was the way we had encouraged self-help, and people's ability to fight back in deprived communities.'

■ December 1992 The President poses for a group photograph with members of GLEN (Gay and Lesbian Equality Network) at Áras an Uachtaráin.

April 1992 President Robinson at Áras an Uachtaráin with members of INOU, the Irish National Organisation of the Unemployed.

■ August 1993 Five-year-old Jennifer Garde from Cork meets the President when children suffering from cystic fibrosis visited Áras an Uachtaráin.

April 1991 The President accepting a drawing by pupils of third class in Scoil Naomh Pádraigh when she opened the 'Playground in the Park' in Mallow, Co. Cork.

■ July 1993 Scouts from Enniskillen welcome President Robinson to the opening of the Ballyfin '93 International Scouts Jamboree at Ballyfin House, Co. Laois.

May 1993 President Robinson on Inishbofin, Co. Galway to visit Inishbofin Arts Week. Pictured with her is Margaret Murray, proprietor of the Doonnure Hotel. The President celebrated her 49th birthday on the island.

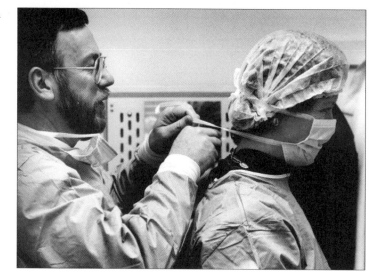

■ February 1993 Assisted by Chief Technologist Tony Finch, President Robinson dons a mask and gown before entering the Eyebank at Pelican House, Dublin. She is a patron of the Irish Fight for Sight Campaign and visited the national cornea donation bank where the 500th cornea for transplantation was being processed.

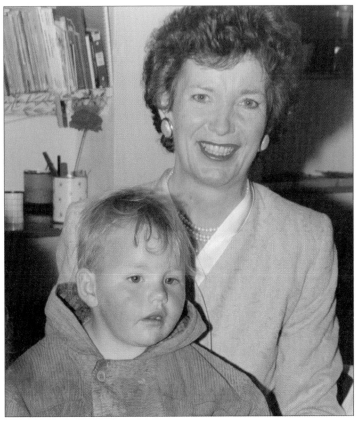

J uly 1994 President Robinson with Lisa Maria Williamson when she met members of the travelling community during a visit to Clonakilty, Co. Cork.

■ May 1992 Having climbed the high tower of St Mary's Cathedral in Limerick, President Robinson has a panoramic view of new developments in Limerick city, as well as familiar historic landmarks.

December 1990 President-elect Mary Robinson visits Pavee Point to address the Travellers' Conference. It was her last public engagement before her inauguration: 'The travelling community is very special to me over a long number of years,' she told the symposium on Travellers, North and South. She was the only non-traveller on the platform. In the society she wanted to represent, she said, 'we must ensure that everyone has a right to a way of life and a culture that is right for them.'

■ June 1992 President Robinson and Nick Robinson vote in the Maastricht referendum, at St Joseph's National School in the Phoenix Park.

May 1993 Celebrating the start of Age and Opportunity Week, President Robinson attends an inter-faith service entitled 'Joining Forces — Young and Old for Peace' at the Royal Hospital Kilmainham, Dublin.

■ January 1994 President Robinson behind the controls of an Aer Lingus Boeing 737 jet when she visited the Microsoft stand at the Aer Lingus Young Scientist Exhibition at the Royal Dublin Society. She was supervised by pilot Tina Murray as she 'flew' the simulator.

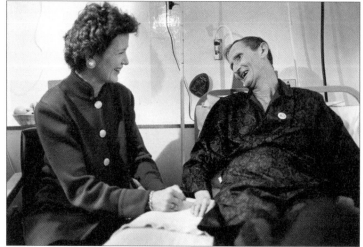

January 1994 President Robinson at the launch of the 'Rinn Voyager', the first steel boat to be built in Dublin port for 40 years. The boat was built by trainees from Ringsend Community Workshop and pictured here is Michelle Ryan from Fenian Street, the only woman involved in the building of the boat.

■ February 1993 President Robinson meets Bill Walsh, a heart transplant patient in the Cardiac Unit of the Mater Hospital, to help promote the Heartbeats Club, a support organisation for Ireland's heart transplant patients.

June 1993 'Me Auld Flower': President Robinson being given a cheery greeting during her visit to Ballymun to launch the Ballymun Partnership, an organisation tackling local unemployment. This photograph, by Mick Slevin, won a special award for the most humorous picture in the Eircell press photography awards of 1993.

■ January 1992 A well-wisher grasps the President's hands as she arrives in Ennis, Co. Clare to visit the 'Le Dúil sa Dúchas' exhibition at the de Valera Library.

July 1991 President Robinson performing the official opening of a new housing development by the Douglas Old Folks Housing Association and the Douglas and District Lions Club in Cork.

J uly 1991 Rows of school-children line the footpath to greet President Robinson and her husband Nick in Passage West, Co. Cork where she performed the official opening of the new town centre. Charlie Hennessy, chairman of Passage West Town Commissioners, walks on her right.

■ April 1991 At the Sheltered Care Project in Charleville, Co. Cork President Robinson shakes hands with Mary O'Donovan (91) while her sister Lena looks on.

November 1993 President Robinson opening the Silver Jubilee Conference of the Irish Wildbird Conservancy, commemorating its 25th anniversary. On the right is Sparky, the organisation's mascot.

■ May 1994 At the opening of Ireland's first Famine museum at Strokestown Park House, Co. Roscommon President Robinson listens to Jim Callery of the Westward Group, which purchased and restored the property and funded half the cost of the museum.

November 1993 After her official opening of an apartment complex for SHARE in Cork, President Robinson meets some of the students involved in the organisation. SHARE was set up in 1970 by the students of Presentation College, Cork and now involves over 2,000 students from more than 20 schools around the city. It was the organisation's 200th project for the elderly in Cork.

■ May 1994 President Robinson talks to Rose Mooney during her visit to the National League of the Blind in Ireland at Gardiner Place, Dublin.

November 1990 President-elect Robinson during her visit to St Joseph's National School, East Wall Road in Dublin.

■ June 1993 President Robinson with members of the Irish Red Cross (of which she is President) at a garden party at Áras an Uachtaráin where she presented their annual awards.

D ecember 1991 President Robinson gets a laugh at the Beara Community College, Allihies, Co. Cork where she had started her election campaign in May 1990.

■ March 1992 President Robinson with the Mother Abbess of the Poor Clare Convent at Nuns Island, Galway. The order was celebrating the 350th anniversary of their arrival in Galway. This was the first visit by a President to an enclosed order of nuns.

THE

FAMILY

A rare photograph of the Robinsons together in the garden of their Dublin home in Ranelagh before they took up residence in Áras an Uachtaráin. This house was later sold. Seated left to right with the President and her husband Nick are their children, Tessa (21), William (20) and Aubrey (12) with Tiger, their retriever. President Robinson has guarded the family privacy, sheltering her children from the spotlight of constant media attention.

The Robinson household is one in which everyone is expected to play their part, the President told *Image* magazine. Mary Robinson's own family background was one where equality between herself and her four brothers was taken for granted and it was her mother, Tessa, who encouraged her daughter to study law. Tessa O'Donnell from the Inishowen Peninsula, Co. Donegal had been a doctor practising on the Aran Islands when she met and married Mary's father, Aubrey Bourke, a doctor in Ballina, Co. Mayo. She died in 1974. Dr Aubrey Bourke was an active supporter of his daughter's election campaign and they remain very close.

The President's husband Nick, once described as 'the perfect consort', is constantly by her side. A graduate of Trinity College, Dublin where he met his future wife, Nick Robinson comes from a family who were originally barrel makers in Dublin's Liberties in the nineteenth century. A cartoonist in London and later with *The Irish Times* in Dublin, Nick Robinson practised as a solicitor in his own law firm and was a full-time administrator of the Irish Centre for European Law at Trinity College, which he co-founded with his wife. In the mid-1970s he co-founded the Irish Architectural Association. A constant and good humoured source of support and encouragement for his wife, he once told an interviewer that 'people like to see a man supporting a woman.'

All the young Robinsons are still studying. Tessa, their daughter, is a student at Trinity College, Dublin while William is at university in Scotland. Aubrey, the youngest, is still a schoolboy at Sandford Park School in Dublin.

Holding hands with her father, Dr Aubrey Bourke, after her election victory.

■ With son Aubrey, tying another knot, during the presidential campaign.

■ Nick Robinson at home in Sandford Road, Ranelagh before the inauguration.

All the family in January 1991 after President Robinson was presented with an honorary Doctor of Laws degree at a ceremony in Dublin Castle. With them is her father, Dr Aubrey Bourke.

■ The Family Retreat — The west of Ireland has a particular place in Mary Robinson's heart for she is a native of Ballina, 'one of the most western towns in the most western province of the most western nation in Europe' as she described it in her inaugural speech. In 1993 the Robinsons bought Massbrook House, a sporting estate on the shores of Lough Conn about fourteen miles from her home town, as a private hideaway. Built in 1900, the ivy and wisteria clad house is set in 120 acres of mature grounds with its own private lakeside jetty.

WELCOME
PRESIDENT ROBINSO
LAUNCH OF NETWORK OF WOMEN'S GROUPS 10 JULY 1991

WOMEN: FROM
PARTICIPATION TO POWER

'As a woman I want women who have felt themselves outside history to be written back into history.' Inaugural address, 3 December 1990

July 1991 President Robinson launches the West of Ireland Network of Women's Groups in Headford, Co. Galway. 'It was a joyous and celebratory occasion which marked the linking of forty-three such groups stretching from Achill to Bohola, Clifden to Letterfrack, Tuam to Galway. It included old and young, traditional and feminist. I can still picture the faces in that packed hall and the shared commitment to valuing what they were doing,' she later recalled.

A long standing champion of women's rights, President Robinson has used her presidency as a platform from which to endorse, validate and listen to women's groups and networks all over Ireland, at every level, from the most margin-alised and remote to the high profile organisations.

Her annual itineraries and schedule of engagements are an eloquent testimony to the enormous proliferation of such groups (nearly 500 applied for grants in 1992) and their increasing sense of empowerment. Her election success in itself was a huge psychological victory for 'mná na hÉireann' who 'instead of rocking the cradle, rocked the system,' she said in her joyful acceptance speech. Many who voted for her, she might have added, did both.

Again and again, President Robinson has stressed both in words and in her actions the value of women's creativity and distinctive style of organisation, as a major resource to be cherished. Whether she is visiting a women's refuge in Dublin or a new breast cancer screening unit in Galway, talking to travellers or addressing the Council for the Status of Women, President Robinson has become a potent and formidable symbol of Irish womanhood today, both at home and abroad.

'The cause of women is inseparable from the cause of humanity itself,' she told the audience at Berkeley University in California in October 1991. The following year in a major lecture entitled 'Striking a Balance', she emphasised again the need to look at 'the work of women, the views of women, their way of organising and their interpretation of social priorities', to make real progress in equality.

July 1991 A man's work is never done: preparing for the President's visit to Headford, Co. Galway. 'What does the President coming to Headford mean? It means that the Town Hall is finished and the clock is working for the first time in years,' Paul O'Grady, chairman of the Chamber of Commerce told *The Irish Times.*

■ March 1994 At the UN Forum on Women's Leadership in New York, where President Robinson received a standing ovation. In her address she said that 'equality in the workplace, in public life and in the home had to stress the wider benefits for men and society as a whole.'

December 1990 President-elect Mary Robinson with Frances Fitzgerald, chairwoman of the Council for the Status of Women, at the delegate meeting held by the Council in response to her election victory. Mrs Robinson was presented with a picture by artist Pauline Cummins.

■ January 1991 President Robinson launches the Women of Europe Award in Dublin.

October 1991 President Robinson greets President Vigdis Finnbogadottir of Iceland on her arrival at Dublin Airport for her first state visit to Ireland. 'It was a particular pleasure,' said President Robinson, 'to greet the world's first democratically elected woman head of state.'

■ December 1992 Celebrating women's achievements: President Robinson appointing Mrs Justice Susan Gageby Denham as Ireland's first female Supreme Court judge.

ovember 1990 At the Women's Political Association (WPA) annual conference, President-elect Mary Robinson told the 400-strong audience that the strongest impression from her campaign trail was the self-development of women in both rural and urban areas. 'That is the beginning of a very real change in this country,' she said.

■ May 1993 President Robinson leaves the headquarters of the ATGWU (Amalgamated Transport and General Workers' Union) in Dublin having performed the official opening of the union's first women's conference.

June 1992 Opening Stanhope Green Housing Project for Focus Point, an organisation which helps young homeless people. President Robinson is seen here with Sister Stanislaus Kennedy, activist and campaigner, and director of Focus Point.

■   February 1994 President Robinson welcoming members of the Northern Ireland Council for Voluntary Action to Áras an Uachtaráin. From left: Quentin Oliver, member of the Council of State and director of NICVA; Roisín McDonagh, NICVA; Paschal McKeown, MENCAP; Patricia Morgan, Anti-Poverty Network.

March 1991 President Robinson at the Women's Aid refuge in Rathmines, Dublin. The refuge was celebrating its fifth anniversary on the day that the President herself had completed 100 days in office.

■ December 1991 A group from the Wexford Ladies' Club with President Robinson at Áras an Uachtaráin.

HONOURS AND AWARDS

ary Robinson, Born 21 May 1944, Ballina, Co. Mayo
Married 1970, Nicholas Robinson
Three children: Tessa, William and Aubrey

THIRD LEVEL EDUCATION

Dublin University	B.A. (1st class Moderatorship) 1967
(Trinity College)	M.A. 1970
	LL.B. (1st class) 1967
King's Inns, Dublin	Degree of Barrister at Law (1st class) 1967
Harvard University	Fellowship 1967
	LL.M. (1st class) 1968

OCCUPATION AND APPOINTMENTS

President of Ireland 1990–

Senator 1969–89

Barrister 1967

Senior Counsel 1980

Member of the English Bar (Middle Temple) 1973

Founder and Director, Irish Centre of European Law 1988–90

Reid Professor of Constitutional and Criminal Law, Trinity College, Dublin 1969–75

Lecturer in European Community Law, TCD 1975–90

Member, Editorial Board of *Irish Current Law Statutes Annotated* 1984–90

Member, Irish Parliamentary Joint Committee on EC Secondary Legislation 1973–89

    Chairman of its Social Affairs Sub-Committee 1977–87

    Chairman of its Legal Affairs Committee 1987–89

Member, Dublin City Council 1979–83

Member, New Ireland Forum 1983–84

President of CHERISH, the Irish association of single parents 1973–90

Member, Irish Parliamentary Joint Committee on Marital Breakdown 1983–85

Member, Vedel Committee, EC (Enlargement of European Parliament) 1971–72

Member, Saint-Geours Committee, EC (Energy Efficiency) 1978–79

Member, Advisory Board of *Common Market Law Review* 1976–90

Member, Advisory Committee of Interights, London 1984–90

Member, International Commission of Jurists, Geneva 1987–90

Member of the Committee of Management, European Air Law Association 1989–90

Member of the Scientific Council of *European Review of Public Law* 1989–90

Member of Chambers, 2 Hare Court, London 1989–90

Member of Euro Avocats, Brussels, 1989–90

General Rapporteur, 'Human Rights at the Dawn of the 21st Century', Council of
   Europe, Strasbourg, 1993

HONOURS AND AWARDS

Member, Royal Irish Academy

Doctor of Laws by Diploma: Oxford

Doctor of Laws (*honoris causa*): National University of Ireland; Cambridge; Brown;
   Liverpool; Dublin; Montpellier; St Andrew's; Melbourne; Columbia; National
   University of Wales; Poznan; Toronto

Honorary Bencher, King's Inns, Dublin; Middle Temple, London

Honorary Fellow, Trinity College, Dublin

Honorary Fellow, Institution of Engineers of Ireland

Honorary Fellow, Royal College of Physicians of Ireland

Honorary Fellow, Royal College of Psychiatrists, London

Honorary Fellow, Hertford College, Oxford

Honorary Fellow, Royal College of Surgeons, Ireland

Freedom of the City of Cork

Berkeley Medal, University of California

Medal of Honour, University of Coimbra, Portugal

Medal of Honour, Ordem dos Advogados, Portugal

Gold Medal of Honour, University of Salamanca, Spain

Marisa Bellisario Prize, Italy, 1991

European Media Prize, Netherlands, 1991

Special Humanitarian Award, CARE, Washington, 1993

International Human Rights Award, International League of Human Rights,
   New York, 1993

Liberal International Prize for Freedom, 1993

New Zealand Suffrage Centennial Medal, 1993

Honorary Doctorate in Public Service, North Eastern University, Boston, 1994

Max Schmidheiny Foundation Freedom Prize for 1994

February 1992 President Robinson's historic first visit to Belfast where, as a guest of the Women's Support Network and the Women's European Platform, she attended a reception hosted by the Equal Opportunities Commission. She said later that she had 'a sense of great sadness that people feel so trapped in their situation that violence may seem like a way of responding and a possible solution.'

NORTHERN IRELAND: THE HAND OF FRIENDSHIP

'Of all the occasions of my presidency, I do not think that any has moved me more than the visits I made to Northern Ireland and the visits made in turn to me by [people] from Northern Ireland.'
Address to the Houses of the Oireachtas, July 1992

A Catholic married to a Protestant, Mary Robinson is deeply committed to mutual understanding between the two communities. In 1985 she resigned from the Labour Party because the Anglo-Irish Agreement, which the Labour Party supported, failed to take account of the Unionist view.

She was the first Irish President to make Northern Ireland an important part of her programme and to welcome both Protestants and Catholics from Belfast to Áras an Uachtaráin. In goodwill visits and in forging links, she sees hope for dialogue and 'a balanced real peace'.

Her visits to the north have been surrounded by controversy. The first, to Belfast in February 1992 when she met a variety of women's and community groups, took place against a backdrop of violence claiming four lives in the course of an afternoon. The 'Adams handshake' in June 1993 caused a political furore.

Abroad she has spoken in positive terms of the prospects for peace: on receiving the International Prize for Freedom in Budapest, President Robinson praised the work of the Belfast Women's Network, which she said had reached across formidable divisions and barriers. Her optimism may be borne out by current positive moves towards peace and the IRA ceasefire announced in September. Time will tell.

February 1991 President Robinson with Jim Rodgers, manager of the Shankill Community Project and chairman of the East Belfast Unionist Association, with six of the Project's young trainees on their visit to Áras an Uachtaráin. Jim Rodgers invited President Robinson to the Shankill.

■ September 1992 President Robinson with four former hostages at the 'Beyond Hate' Conference at Derry Guild Hall. From left: Father Lawrence Jenco, Terry Anderson, Terry Waite and Brian Keenan. This international conference on conflict resolution organised by Derry Centre for Creative Communications was boycotted by the DUP Mayor of

Derry, William Hay. President Robinson told the conference that peace 'requires the development of a climate of justice and tolerance where diversity can be accommodated, where minds are open — the fifth province — and where change and development are not seen as threats.'

June 1993
Extending the hand of friendship: President Robinson meets the public in Coalisland, Co. Tyrone after officially opening the Coalisland Heritage Centre. She later told them, 'You are a community that works so well together cross-community and I think this building in a symbolic way reflects what can be achieved when we work well together.'

■ Protest outside Coalisland Heritage Centre. Former MP Bernadette McAliskey staged a placard protest on behalf of a number of families of people killed in sectarian violence.

June 1993 West Belfast: Tight security for the President's visit to the Rupert Stanley College in Whiterock Road.

■ June 1993 West Belfast: The President watches an Irish dancer before an audience which included musicians, schoolchildren, teachers, trade unionists and community workers at the Rupert Stanley College. The President was a guest of six West Belfast community organisations in an area greatly marked by twenty years of violence. Gerry Adams, the Sinn Féin president, can be seen in the audience, and it was on this occasion, at a private reception for community leaders, that the controversial handshake between Mr Adams and President Robinson took place.

October 1993 President Robinson with Prince Charles at the launch of the Warrington Peace Project, a one-day seminar aimed at increasing community contact between Ireland and Britain. This followed the deaths, by an IRA bomb in Warrington, of Tim Parry (12) and Jonathan Ball (3). The President spoke of the 'great moral authority' on which the people of Warrington could draw when they made 'a common possession of their suffering and a common purpose of their healing'. The visit of the Prince was only made known a few hours beforehand and a private meeting between him and the President lasted about 7 minutes. The day concluded with a reading of a poem by John Hewitt which was dedicated to the families of the two Warrington boys and to the families of all the victims of violence on these islands over the past 25 years.

March 1994 The President on a one-day visit to Newry and Craigavon to mark the 850th anniversary of the foundation of the town of Newry. The visit was preceded by contention over the nature of the visit when Unionist MP Mr David Trimble claimed that Mrs Robinson was 'deliberately insulting the Queen and her loyal subjects in Ulster with an itinerary more suitable for a public visit'. President Robinson described it as 'a working visit in the best sense'.

■ Surrounded by security men, the President arrives at Craigavon to

inspect the work of the Brownlow Community Trust, an organisation working towards the regeneration of locally deprived areas.

President Robinson smiles as her husband Nick tries his hand at plasticine with a group of three-year-olds from Monbrief Playgroup, Craigavon, on their visit to the Brownlow Centre.

FIRST CITIZEN:
AT HOME AND ABROAD

The first four years of Mary Robinson's presidency have been characterised by extensive and unprecedented travel abroad as Ireland's first citizen. She has used these trips to present a new face of Ireland to the world, that of a young and modern European nation, as well as fostering important social, political, cultural and economic links across several continents.

Since her inauguration, President Robinson has travelled widely in the EU member states, to Portugal, Spain, France, Holland and Germany, as well as to other European countries such as Norway and Switzerland. Her state visit to Poland was the first to any of the former communist countries of central and eastern Europe. There have been three trips to the US, one to Canada, state visits to New Zealand and India with a visit to Hong Kong in between as well as state visits to Zambia, Zimbabwe and Tanzania. She was the first Irish President in office to visit England, Scotland and Wales, and her meeting with Queen Elizabeth was an occasion which broke new ground in relations between the two countries. Within ten days of another ground breaking trip, to Somalia, she departed on a state visit to Australia, visiting all the major cities in an exhaustive two-week itinerary.

Much in demand by overseas organisations and institutions because of her reputation as a champion of civil liberties, her active foreign schedules also reflect her interest in foreign affairs and human rights as well as her desire to keep in touch with Irish communities abroad.

On home soil, she has hosted several state visits as well as attending to her formal 'household' duties of welcoming and bidding farewell to high-ranking diplomats or visiting dignitaries. As Ireland's most active head of state, she has in fact become her country's premier ambassador.

March 1993 President Robinson shows actor Paul Newman around the grounds of Áras an Uachtaráin. His 'Hole in the Wall Gang' charity funded a £5 million American-style holiday project in Ireland for seriously ill children.

■ July 1992 President von Weizsacker of the Federal Republic of Germany on the first day of his state visit to Ireland, planting a tree at Áras an Uachtaráin. Recalling his visit later that year, President Robinson drew comparisons between his symbolic role and her own, saying that he had found 'ways of conveying the importance of respect, and inclusion of all the components of Germany after reunification, on a basis of mutual understanding and respect'.

arch 1994 US Senator Ted Kennedy, who hosted a breakfast for President Robinson and 400 other guests, presenting her with a set of President John F. Kennedy's collected speeches when she visited the John F. Kennedy Presidential Library in Boston.

■ June 1993 President Robinson with the Portuguese President, Dr Mario Soares, on board the *L. E. Eithne* in Cork Harbour during his state visit to Ireland. Also present are Captain John Kavanagh, Commanding Officer, Naval Service and Lieutenant General Noel Bergin, Army COS.

■ May 1994 Dr Thomas Klestil, President of Austria, being welcomed by President Mary Robinson and her husband Nick in the grounds of Áras an Uachtaráin.

June 1991 President Robinson chatting with Mr Ali Said Mchumo after he presented his credentials as Ambassador of the United Republic of Tanzania.

■ March 1994 President Robinson shares a joke with Harvard University undergraduates as she began a two-day visit to the university where she herself was a postgraduate student from 1967–68.

Seeptember 1993 At a colourful ceremony in Rashrapati Bhavan, the presidential palace in New Delhi, President Robinson is welcomed by Indian Prime Minister P. V. Narasimha Rao on her state visit to India.

■ September 1993 President Robinson with Mother Teresa of Calcutta, the 82-year-old Nobel Peace Prize winner who brought her on a tour of her children's orphanage in Calcutta. Later the President opened a centre for street children which was partly funded by the Irish relief and development agency, GOAL.

■ September 1993 President Robinson admires carvings on the walls of ruins around the 13th century Qutab Minar, a huge tower in New Delhi, during her official visit. She also visited the grave of Mahatma Gandhi, the country's passive resistance leader, who has always been one of her heroes. The Indian visit was of special significance for her personally as her aunt, Mother Ivy Bourke, spent thirty years in India as a nun.

February 1992 President Robinson at the England vs. Ireland rugby international at Twickenham as a guest of the Rugby Football Union. Alongside her are British Prime Minister, John Major, and the South African President, F. W. de Klerk.

■ March 1994 President Robinson with former British Prime Minister, Lord James Callaghan, during his visit to Áras an Uachtaráin.

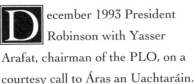

December 1993 President Robinson with Yasser Arafat, chairman of the PLO, on a courtesy call to Áras an Uachtaráin.

■ June 1993 Mother Teresa of Calcutta on a private visit to Áras an Uachtaráin to meet President Robinson. Mother Teresa was in Ireland to receive the Freedom of Dublin and to visit Knock shrine and Northern Ireland.

■ September 1993 President Robinson receiving a *hongi*, the traditional Maori greeting of rubbing noses, from a Maori elder at a *roturua marae* (meeting place) during her state visit to New Zealand. During speeches by her hosts, President Robinson was referred to as 'the white heron' which in Maori belief denotes a leader of a nation. President Robinson was in New Zealand to celebrate the centenary of women's suffrage. It was the first nation to give women the vote in 1893. She spoke to the Maoris of pride in cultural heritage. 'Like you we have a rich oral tradition of song, story and lore handed down by word of mouth.'

June 1991 President Robinson being received by An Taoiseach Charles J. Haughey, as she arrived at Dublin Airport for her departure on a four-day state visit to Portugal, the first by an Irish head of state to that country. The visit followed controversy over the government's refusal to allow her to deliver the Richard Dimbleby lecture on BBC, a lecture that was to have been on women and public life.

■ October 1992 President Robinson in Sydney, Australia, during her two-week visit to the country in which she toured the major cities of Perth, Sydney, Canberra, Melbourne and Adelaide. In Sydney a crowd of 6,000 people held a spontaneous collection for Somalia. In her speeches she spoke about the historical connection between Ireland and Australia, and said that Ireland was now a modern European nation 'open for business'. She also emphasised that western societies still had not found the right balance on women's rights or fully accepted their responsibilities in alleviating world hunger and deprivation.

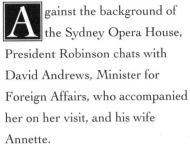

Against the background of the Sydney Opera House, President Robinson chats with David Andrews, Minister for Foreign Affairs, who accompanied her on her visit, and his wife Annette.

■ July 1994 The Prime Minister of Pakistan, Ms Benazir Bhutto and her mother, Ms Nusrat Bhutto, meet President Robinson at Áras an Uachtaráin.

August 1994 President Mary Robinson and Nick Robinson at Dublin Airport before their departure on her official trip to Canada.

■ June 1994 President Robinson on a four-day state visit to Poland is greeted by President Lech Walesa during the welcoming ceremony for her at Belveder, the presidential palace in Warsaw. She said that with a population of 40 million people Poland would, because of its size and significance, play a leading role in the development of the European economy.

M
ay 1993 President Robinson with President Bill Clinton in the Oval Office of the White House, Washington D.C. Her invitation to the White House was seen as a tribute to her international standing.

■   May 1994 President Robinson and Ruairí Quinn, Minister of Enterprise and Employment, with President Nelson Mandela of South Africa in the grounds of his residence in Pretoria, following his inauguration.

A TYPICAL

WEEK

resident Robinson's Engagements
Week commencing Monday 30 March 1992

TUESDAY 31 MARCH

10.00 a.m.   President Robinson receives Ambassador Juliette C. McLennan.

10.40 a.m.   Train departs for Limerick.

1.15 p.m.   Limerick Ryan Hotel

President Robinson has lunch with members of Limerick Chamber of Commerce.

2.30 p.m.   96 O'Connell Street, Limerick

President Robinson visits the offices of Limerick Chamber of Commerce.

3.30 p.m.   President Robinson attends a private engagement in Limerick.

6.00 p.m.   University of Limerick

President Robinson attends the opening of the Joint Sessions of the European Consortium for Political Research.

THURSDAY 2 APRIL

10.30 a.m.   European Foundation, Loughlinstown House, Shankill

President Robinson opens a seminar for the 'Exchange of Information and Experiences on the Problem of Alcohol' which is being held by the Irish Countrywomen's Association in conjunction with COFACE.

12.00 noon   President Robinson receives a group of postgraduate European business students from the European School of Management.

1.00 p.m.   President Robinson receives Edward L. Lawlor of the Lawlor Foundation.

3.00 p.m.   President Robinson receives members of the Ruckert Chamber Orchestra and members of the Active Retirement Association of Dun Laoghaire.

FRIDAY 3 APRIL

10.30 a.m.	Interview with Lisa Carlsson for Swedish television.
11.30 a.m.	President Robinson receives pupils of St Paul's High School, Newry, and Our Lady's Bower, Athlone.
1.00 p.m.	President Robinson receives Sir A. Lester.
2.30 p.m.	President Robinson receives pupils from Dunshane Training Centre, Naas.
5.00 p.m.	Members of the Donna Club, Cork, call to see the formal rooms of the Áras. (President Robinson will not be receiving them.)
6.00 p.m.	King's Inns, Dublin President Robinson launches the Essays of T. F. O'Higgins.
7.30 p.m. for 8.00 p.m.	The Stephen's Green Club, Dublin President Robinson is a guest for dinner of Mr Justice T. F. O'Higgins and Mrs O'Higgins.

SATURDAY 4 APRIL

10.30 a.m.	Grand Hotel, Malahide, Co. Dublin President Robinson performs the official opening of the Leo Club International conference.
11.30 a.m.	Royal Hospital, Kilmainham, Dublin President Robinson performs the official opening of a conference: 'Cancer — A European Perspective' for the Irish Association of Nurses in Oncology.
1.35 p.m.	Train departs for Wexford.
4.15 p.m.	Talbot Hotel, Wexford President Robinson attends the Congress of the Union of Students of Ireland.
6.26 p.m.	Train departs for Dublin.

SUNDAY 5 APRIL

12.00 noon	'Denmark Hill', Leinster Road West, Dublin President Robinson performs the official opening of the new extension to The Jewish Home of Ireland.
2.45 p.m.	Kenilworth Bowling Club, Dublin President Robinson visits the Club.

HUMAN RIGHTS:

WITNESS AND ADVOCATE

'I would like on your behalf to contribute to the international protection and promotion of human rights.' Inaugural address, 3 December 1990

October 1992 Arriving back in Dublin from the UN, President Robinson's face shows some of the anguish and strain of her visit to Somalia. 'When you have nothing in mind but the humanitarian aspect, you possess a great deal of credibility,' she said.

Few will forget the face of President Robinson fighting back tears as she faced the press in Nairobi after her dramatic visit to Somalia in October 1992, her voice breaking as she described what she had witnessed in the previous three days.

Her presence, the first by any head of state, with its attendant media publicity, served to highlight the plight of 20 million Somali people, facing famine and disease after the devastation of a nineteen-month civil war. Her subsequent appeal at the UN in New York emphasised the urgency of humanitarian aid to alleviate their terrible suffering.

The visit was one of the high points of her first two years in office and served as a powerful reminder of her primary concern, human rights. Internationally recognised as an outstanding civil rights lawyer, Mary Robinson's whole political and legal career can be said to have been driven by a fundamental belief in the rights of the individual in the enactment of legislation. The many awards conferred on her since her inauguration have been a tribute to her particular contribution.

As President, she has acted as both witness and advocate of human rights whether visiting a shelter for homeless boys in Dublin or cradling a dying child in Somalia. In January 1993 at a Council of Europe conference on 'Human Rights at the Dawn of the 21st Century' where she was General Rapporteur, she stressed: 'at the end of the road it is our capacity as individuals to be concerned and moved by injustice that is the real driving force behind the human rights movement. We must ensure that the seeds of such individual responsibilities are firmly planted and nourished in our national cultures.'

October 1992 President Robinson at a feeding centre in Baidoa, Somalia where she was repeatedly told: 'We need medicines, we need clothing. Our children are cold. Please tell the world.'

■ President Robinson shaking hands with the Koran teacher at an orphanage established by the Somali people where GOAL were operating a supplementary feeding centre.

The President cradling a child emaciated from hunger.

■ President Robinson walks with UN Secretary General Boutros Boutros-Ghali in New York after her three-day visit to Somalia. She stressed the need for the urgent deployment of troops to Somalia at the UN. 'I am giving an eyewitness account, not a political account,' she said.

December 1992 With guest speaker Rakiya Omaar, a Somali lawyer, at the launch of *A Voice for Somalia*, President Robinson's diary of her visit to Somalia, in Dublin Castle. Royalties from the sale of the book were donated to Irish aid agencies for use in their work in the Horn of Africa.

■ November 1992 President Robinson with two of the young residents of the Don Bosco House for homeless boys in Blessington Street, Dublin when she officially opened the new premises.

■ October 1992 At a news conference at the UN Headquarters in New York, President Robinson makes a point as she talks to reporters about the situation in Somalia.

March 1994 President Robinson at Harvard University's John F. Kennedy School of Government where she delivered a major speech on the role of the United Nations. Stressing the need to uphold universal human values in a changing world, she said 'we must hold on to what has been achieved in human rights over the last fifty years.' She suggested that connectedness, listening, sharing and participation were fundamental ways of structuring international relations.

■ November 1993 Budapest: President Robinson being awarded the 1993 Freedom Award by Otto Lambsdorf, president of Liberal International, on the first day of the Liberal International Conference. President Robinson was given the award for her active part in human rights cases. In her acceptance speech, she spoke about women's groups in the north of Ireland crossing boundaries and how 'we must repair a sense of powerlessness with a sense of participation.' Hungary was the first eastern European country to embrace democracy and to secure membership of the Council of Europe.

December 1992 President Mary Robinson with Fatima Sinandvic during her visit to the Bosnian refugee centre at Dublin's Cherry Orchard.

■ October 1991 President Robinson acknowledges applause after her address to the University of California at Berkeley watched by Cheng-Lin Tien, its Chancellor. President Robinson spoke of the widening gap between the developing and developed worlds and the importance of imaginative concern for human anguish wherever it occurs.

October 1991 Arriving at the Grand Hotel, Malahide to open a Barnardos seminar entitled 'A Window on Irish Children', President Robinson is greeted by Owen Keenan, secretary of Barnardos and Dr Joseph Robins, chairman.

■ May 1993 Washington D.C.: In front of a photograph taken in Bangladesh, President Mary Robinson listens to a speech made by Warren Christopher, US Secretary of State, who presented her with the CARE Humanitarian Award for her efforts in Somalia. CARE is a charitable relief operation. Describing her as an 'invaluable advocate of the people of Somalia', Mr Christopher said that 'her heroic efforts ... helped awaken the world's conscience.' President Robinson dedicated the award to two Irish aid workers who were killed in Somalia.

O ctober 1992 At a feeding centre in Baidoa President Robinson sees first-hand the suffering of the Somali people. Later, at the UN in New York, she told reporters, 'I feel completely shamed and diminished when I see fellow citizens of this world ... deprived of even the right to life or any quality of life.'

■ September 1993 During her visit to a centre for battered women and children in Calcutta funded by GOAL, President Robinson paid particular tribute to Edith Wilkins (right), a volunteer from Cork, who had rescued hundreds of children from a life of destitution on the streets. The centre was caring for 2,000 children at the time.

June 1993 At Áras an Uachtaráin, President Robinson with Bosnian and Croatian women who were attending a training course with the Dublin Rape Crisis Centre.

January 1994 With President Mitterrand during the Five Nations Rugby Championship match at Parc des Princes Stadium in Paris. A fluent French speaker, President Robinson is said to have a particularly warm relationship with the French President whom she has met on several occasions. Referring to the match, she said she had talked to President Mitterrand about the friendship between Ireland and France: 'I told him that if it's an open friendship then Ireland will win. He replied that the friendship was suspended until the end of the afternoon.' France defeated Ireland 35–15.

EUROPE: 'SOFT WAX'

Taking an image once used by W. B. Yeats to describe a momentous juncture in Ireland's history, President Robinson likens present-day Europe to 'soft wax', still capable of being shaped and moulded, where the pace of change is rapidly accelerating and new vistas and prospects are opening up.

After Ireland's vote in favour of the Maastricht Treaty on European political and economic union, she used the opportunity to make an address to the Oireachtas (houses of Parliament). In this she reflected not only on the future shape of Europe, but on 'how we shape ourselves within it ... self-definition at a time of redefinition'. It was Ireland's traditional openness to Europe that enriched its culture and sense of identity, she said in her speech: 'Receptive-ness to change is a mark of a nation's confidence.'

Her expertise in and practise of European law have made her aware of the legal possibilities of integration. Ireland is the only one of the twelve member states to combine a common law tradition with a written constitution and she regards the Irish legal system as responding well to the significance of community law as an integrating force. 'It is a legal bridge to other English-speaking jurisdictions such as the US, Canada and Australia.'

Membership of the European Union frees Ireland from defining itself solely in relation to Britain, helps in discussions on Northern Ireland as well as bringing clear economic, psychological and cultural benefits; these are points she has often stressed. She has visited many of the European Union member states, each time using the occasion to recall historical links with the country concerned as well as promoting Ireland as a modern European nation.

June 1993 Schoolgirls from the Bom Sucesso convent in Lisbon, which was established in 1639 by a Co. Kerry priest, line up to greet President Robinson during her state visit to Portugal in 1991.

■ April 1992 At Het Low Palace in Holland, President Robinson receives the European Media Prize for her contribution to European integration. She was the first woman and the first Irish person to be awarded the prize. She later donated the £4,000 prize money to FLAC (Free Legal Advice Centres) for its work in highlighting European welfare rights in Ireland. She is pictured here with Dr Pierre

Meyrat of Switzerland (left), Mr Pieter van Vollenhoven, Hon. President of the Dutch branch of the European Journalists Association (right) and Edgar Morin of France (far right).

December 1992 President Robinson with her husband Nick and Tom Kitt, Minister of State at the Department of the Environment, at the Brandenburg Gate before touring East Berlin. The President was a guest of the Berlin Press Club.

■ May 1992 As guest of honour at a lavish banquet hosted by President and Madame Mitterrand in the Elysée Palace, Paris, President Robinson reminded guests of the long-standing links between Ireland and France.

May 1993 The Royal Palace, Madrid: At a gala dinner in her honour, President Robinson with Spain's King Juan Carlos. 'Ireland would never forget the assistance Spain had given Irish refugees over the centuries,' President Robinson said in her address to a select group of 100 guests drawn from the top echelons of Spanish society.

■ May 1993 With great pomp and ceremony, President Robinson inspects a mounted guard of honour in Madrid accompanied by the Mayor of Madrid, José Alvarez del Manzano, during her three-day state visit to the country. Outside the

courtyard of City Hall about 200 striking street cleaners staged a demonstration and had to be kept back by riot police as the President reviewed the City Hall lancers.

BEHIND THE SCENES:
HOW IT WORKS

The total cost of the Irish presidency (as of September 1994) to the Irish tax payer is an estimated £1,784,000 a year which includes the President's salary of £105,512. There are nine full-time employees on the household staff and twelve on the administrative/secretarial side. Four army officers rotate the job of aide-de-camp including Captain Colette Harrison, the first woman ever to hold the position. Responsibility for the maintenance of Áras an Uachtaráin and the surrounding gardens and parkland lies with the Office of Public Works (OPW).

President Robinson begins her working day around 7 a.m. when she makes breakfast for her family. She also uses this time to catch up on news and current affairs as she usually has no appointments before 10 a.m. In the evenings she tries whenever possible, to have supper with her family and friends. The smooth operation of the President's busy schedule is facilitated by two key individuals: Bride Rosney, her special adviser and Peter Ryan, her secretary.

Each week upwards of 100 invitations are received at the Áras. In the first year of her presidency she accepted twenty-five per cent of all invitations but the volume has increased so substantially over the years that she now has to turn down eighty-five per cent of them. Nonetheless, she still averages a daily schedule of four to five engagements. Invitations given priority are those which reflect the themes of her presidency and any that serve to improve or strengthen north/south ties are given immediate precedence. Acceptances are always 'subject to state business commitments' and in general terms, she is booked up three to four months in advance. During her first three years of office she fulfilled more than 2,100 public engagements both at home and abroad.

On her trips abroad, which she prefers to call 'working visits', the President often initiates her own activities around an anchor event, such as accepting an award or delivering an address. She prepares her speeches from written briefs compiled for her in advance, but she speaks without notes. Less than ten per cent of her speeches are scripted for her. One of her more onerous tasks is the reading of government bills which can be upwards of 100 pages in length. She has regular meetings with the Taoiseach every 5–6 weeks at the Áras and in her first four years of office she has called the Council of State together four times. In February 1995 she is scheduled to give the keynote address in Strasbourg, at the Council of Europe's preparatory meeting for the UN Conference on Women, due to take place in Beijing in September 1995. There are also tentative plans for state visits to Argentina and Chile.

S eptember 1991 At the Ladies
Camogie Final in Croke Park, the
President looks on as Angela Downey,
outgoing captain of the winning Kilkenny
team and recognised as the most
outstanding camogie player of the decade,
embraces Biddy O'Sullivan, her full back.
It was the first time any President had
attended the Ladies Camogie Final.

Irish Culture:
Language, Sport, the Arts

Pride in heritage, culture and in the native language itself has been a recurring motif of Mary Robinson's presidency. Her first public commitment was to the Irish language when she pledged to relearn it. It was a note of optimism in a country where less than five per cent of the population use Irish as their principal language.

Her presidency has coincided with a cultural renaissance in Ireland of all the arts and many sporting triumphs, bringing with them a new bravado and sense of confidence in national identity. In music, art, drama, literature and film, Irish artists are making names worldwide. In her Allen Lane Foundation Lecture in 1992, President Robinson said 'we have a powerful culture, a literature which celebrates it, a balance between tradition and the contemporary which many nations would give a great deal to have.'

She has also spoken about the unifying nature of sport. Her many appearances at sporting and artistic events pay tribute not only to her keen interest and support but also to the level of activity and creativity in the country at large. One of the themes of her presidency is to promote excellence in all its forms. On state visits, for example, she has always brought Irish-made gifts; to the White House a wooden vessel by Peter Sweetman, to President Nelson Mandela of South Africa, a silver candelabra made by the silversmith Kevin O'Dwyer, to the Queen of England a hand-turned wooden bowl by Liam O'Neill, celebrating a tradition in Ireland of woodturning going back 3,000 years.

Preservation of the environment is another concern and she is patron of organisations dedicated to conservation as well as an ardent advocate of local initiative projects in aquaculture, forestry, fishing, alternative energy and small scale technology to which she referred in her inaugural speech. These achievements great or small to which she is witness, the major as well as the minor endeavours, are part of 'the telling of stories of celebration' which she promised.

May 1991 Dressed in green and white, President Robinson with members of the Irish soccer team before the Ireland vs. Poland match.

■ December 1991 In the midst of controversy over the siting of interpretative centres in various parts of the country, President Robinson officially opened the Dublin Institute of Architecture Winter School at the Bolton Street College of Technology. She reminded architects of the necessity to avoid arrogance, and of their duty to remain in harmony with the environment. Seated is college principal Mr Michael O'Donnell.

September 1991 At the All-Ireland Football Final in Croke Park where Down beat Meath, a victorious captain Paddy O'Rourke holds high the Sam Maguire cup, applauded by President Robinson.

■ September 1992 A jubilant Liam Fennelly, captain of the winning Kilkenny team, with the Liam McCarthy cup at the Kilkenny vs. Cork All-Ireland Senior Hurling Final in Croke Park.

August 1991 The President with the Papal Nuncio and members of the diplomatic corps at the opening of the Aga Khan Nations Cup at the RDS Horse Show. She was a guest of Dervilla Donnelly, president of the Royal Dublin Society and her escort, Dr Herman Frolich.

■ February 1991 President Robinson arrives at the Savoy Cinema, Dublin to open the sixth Dublin Film Festival. Also in attendance that evening were the Irish film director Neil Jordan and the Oscar-winning Irish actress Brenda Fricker. In her speech, the President expressed her deep interest and support for film and film makers and said that she rejoiced in the vitality and success of Irish film in recent years.

April 1992 The President and her husband Nick accompany King Gustav and Queen Silvia of Sweden to Staigue Fort in Co. Kerry. The Swedish monarchs were on a state visit to Ireland.

■ February 1992 President Robinson at the European Person of the Year Award with its recipient, the celebrated Irish playwright, Brian Friel. 'The themes which engage him and his audience are so relevant to the Europe of today,' she said.

June 1992 President Robinson with John Teahan, keeper of the Art and Industrial Division at the National Museum, holding the Cloyne Harp. The President heard a recital by a group of young harpists.

■ July 1991 President Robinson with the team representing Ireland at the International Special Olympic Games for the mentally handicapped.

June 1992 President Robinson presents a rosette to Jim Ryall of Castlemartyr, Co. Cork for his supreme champion Charollais bull at the Cork Summer Show.

■ December 1991 President Robinson and her husband Nick share a joke with one of the exhibitors, Yuka Kemlyama, after the official opening of the National Sculpture Factory in Cork.

June 1991 President
Robinson at the
Budweiser Irish Derby —
on a rare occasion
wearing a hat.

■ December 1991
Admiring a piece of
wooden sculpture at the
National Sculpture
Factory in Cork.

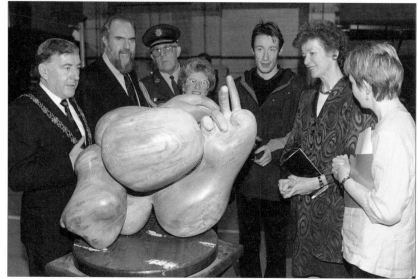

■ June 1993 The President shares a few words with a local resident, the Irish writer Molly Keane, during a visit to Ardmore, Co. Waterford.

■ March 1994 Seamus Heaney at the *Irish Times*/Harvard Colloquium at the John F. Kennedy School of Government, Boston, listening to President Robinson's address on the future of the UN. Later, he told *The Irish Times* that she embodied certain values and that her integrity was such that 'you feel that her endured life and her public life are the same thing. Whatever has been thought out and internalised is part and parcel of her personality. They are the same as her public discourse. The personality that's on view is the personality that's available in her home. That's very unusual in this world.'

J uly 1993 At the launch of the *Irish University Review*, President Robinson paid tribute to her long-standing friendship with the poet, Eavan Boland, to whose work the summer issue was devoted. Recalling their college days, the President said that it was the poet who was the realist and the law student who was the dreamer.

July 1994 President Robinson welcoming the Irish soccer team back home from the World Cup in Orlando, Florida.

■   November 1991 The poet Paul Durcan with President Robinson during her visit to the 'Crazy about Women' exhibition at the National Gallery of Ireland, held to coincide with the publication of his book of poetry of the same title. Afterwards he wrote about the event in *The Sunday Tribune* saying that the President is 'instinctively in touch with other people's feelings.... What amazed me was that she was so involved in and so open to each and every picture and poem.'

May 1993 President Robinson with members of the Irish Everest Expedition team who reached the summit of the Himalayan peak exactly 40 years after Hillery first conquered Everest.

The event coincided with the President's visit to Queen Elizabeth. Referring to the cross-border composition of the team and to Dawson Stelfox, its leader, in particular, who holds both an Irish and British passport, she said she was 'struck by the symbolism of his position and indeed of the whole team'.

■ May 1991 Members of the pop group Hot House Flowers entertain the President round the piano at Áras an Uachtaráin. Afterwards they performed a concert in the Phoenix Park.

The welcome home: a constantly burning light in the kitchen (top left) at Áras an Uachtaráin is a symbolic gesture of welcome to all Irish emigrants.

EMIGRANTS:

HOME AWAY FROM HOME

The most celebrated gesture made by President Robinson shortly after taking up residence in Áras an Uachtaráin was to put a light in her kitchen window. Seen through a gap in the trees, it shines night and day and is her way of symbolising a perpetual welcome for the Irish emigrant and for the extended Irish family around the world. People have wept at the sight of it: Tom Foley, US speaker and Maurice Setters, assistant manager of the Irish soccer team, were both moved to tears when they first saw it.

'I have a certain belief that the light will never go out,' President Robinson told Charlie Bird of RTE in December 1991, 'that it would take a very devastating view of a future President to say "right, we'll put that light out." I don't think it will happen. That light is symbolic of reaching out to the extended Irish family of this island of Ireland, which has lost so many young people. An awful lot of (them) used to say to me that the bitterness was that nobody cared. I think that light signifies that the President of Ireland and the people of Ireland do care.'

Exodus from Ireland has a long history. In this century alone the massive wave of emigration in the 1950s recurred in the 1980s when in one year, 1989, it reached a peak of 46,000 many of them well educated young people. In her election campaign President Robinson vowed that the President's role would be to provide a direct link with these exiles. 'There are over seventy million people living on this globe who claim Irish descent. I will be proud to represent them,' was one of her first promises.

In May 1993 she unveiled a statue in New York commemorating the twelve million emigrants to the US who were processed through Ellis Island. Half a million of these people were Irish and she met a 101-year-old Dublin woman, Elizabeth Scott, who had left Liverpool for Ellis Island at the age of twenty-one. Wherever President Robinson has travelled abroad, to the industrial cities in England, to the US or Australia, she has brought Ireland home to its expatriates, redefining their country in a new and enthusiastic way.

In turn, she has also carried home a message to Ireland, that its emigrants want to retain and strengthen their bonds with their native country, and has suggested exploring ways in which the Irish diaspora can be harnessed to the development of a modern Irish society.

February 1993 President Robinson visiting a replica of a coffin ship from the Irish Famine in the 1840s at Cobh Heritage Project.

March 1994 President Robinson listens to a National Park ranger as she explains the history of the Liberty Bell during a stop on her tour of Philadelphia. At a dinner hosted by the Brehon Law Society of Philadelphia, President Robinson told the guests, many of whom hailed from Mayo, Donegal and Northern Ireland, that she had decided during her presidential campaign to keep a light burning in Áras an Uachtaráin to symbolise her constant thoughts for Irish emigrants and the wider Irish community in the world.

■ April 1994 On a two-day visit to Manchester, President Robinson looks at a booklet about Manchester's Irish Heritage with 82-year-old Anne Conlan, during a tour of the Irish Community Care Centre there.

February 1993 President Robinson unveils a statue in Cobh commemorating Annie Moore, the fifteen-year-old girl from Cork who was the first official immigrant to land when Ellis Island in New York opened in 1892. The sculpture was made by Jeanne Rynhart, a Bantry sculptor. Also in the picture is Anne Belkov, superintendent of the Statue of Liberty on Ellis Island, and Kevin Power, chairman of Cobh UDC. Three months later in New York, the President unveiled another statue of Annie Moore on Ellis Island. Irish emigrants were thus commemorated on both sides of the Atlantic.

■ October 1992 President Robinson receives a gift of an oil painting from Frank Doyle, president of the Celtic Club in Melbourne. The President was on a twelve-day visit to this country of seventeen million people, where some six million claim to be of Irish descent including the Prime Minister, Paul Keating.

December 1991 President Robinson being conferred with an honorary degree of Doctor of Laws by Viscount Leverhulme, Chancellor of the University of Liverpool. The President also visited the Institute of Irish Studies. Over half a million Irish left Ireland for Liverpool during the Famine years and today one-third of the population claims Irish descent.

■ September 1993 In Christchurch, New Zealand President Robinson receives a bouquet of flowers from Donna Maree Brady, an Irish dancer at the Irish Society Hall, during a seven-day tour of New Zealand.

May 1993 President Robinson admires the statue of Annie Moore, during her visit to Ellis Island, New York. With her is John P. Walsh, chairman of the Irish American Institute which sponsored the erection of the statues in Cobh and Ellis Island.

■ May 1993 On her one-week visit to New York and Washington, President Robinson addressed members of the Irish community outside the 'Tír na nÓg' immigration centre in the Bronx.

■ May 1993 President Robinson arriving at the Camden Irish Centre in London's Camden Town where she met representatives of the Irish community prior to visiting the Queen at Buckingham Palace. She was accompanied by the Irish ambassador to Britain, Mr Joe Small. Fr Denis Cormican described her visit to the centre as 'a great source of encouragement'.

A red and white silk dress by Pat Crowley worn by the President on her Australian trip.

■ Stepping out in a red plaid jacket by Pat Crowley.

■ At the Áras, wearing a red wool suit by Louise Kennedy.

A STYLISH FIRST CITIZEN

One of the more noticeable aspects of Mary Robinson's election campaign was the striking change in her style of dress. Almost overnight, lacklustre and rather staid black and navy clothes disappeared and in came smarter, bolder suits and a spanking new hairstyle, a transformation largely masterminded by Cecily McMenamin, director of the Brown Thomas department store in Dublin. In office the President has gradually come to terms with the importance of projecting herself well as a woman and dressing for the part. 'Women take pride in the fact that I look well, but it's not easy,' she once admitted. 'When I'm relaxing, it's jeans and no make-up.' Clothes are simply not an issue for her.

Nevertheless, in 1992 she was voted one of the top twelve best dressed women in the world, a tribute she regards as a recognition of the high standards of the Irish fashion industry since she makes a point of buying and wearing Irish.

Her clothes are chosen for comfort and versatility as the same outfit has often to carry her throughout the day to many different engagements. She still frequently uses Cecily McMenamin to help her assemble the clothes she needs for the various formal and informal functions she must attend at home and particularly for her state visits abroad. The Áras does not give details of her wardrobe. The President does her own make-up and uses the services of local hairdressers.

She buys regularly from Irish designers and manufacturers like Paul Costelloe, Michelina Stacpoole, Jen Kelly, Pat Crowley, Lorcan Mullany, Ib Jorgensen, John McNamara, L.M. Ramsay, Michael Mortell and notably Louise Kennedy, who made her inauguration ensemble. The fuschia suit by Ib Jorgensen which the President wore to meet the Queen of England is now immortalised in Madame Tussaud's Wax Museum in London and a replacement one, in green, was made for her which she later wore at Harvard University. In recent years she has started to wear brighter colours, not only so that she can be distinguished in a crowd, but also because she likes them, a reaction to the more sombre attire she was required to wear in her Law Library days.

Many items are worn again and again: one favourite is a white embroidered jacket by Louise Kennedy, worn in India and on many other occasions. She is also very fond of the knitwear of the Limerick-based designer Michelina Stacpoole. The public love her in short skirts: letters of approval pour in to the Áras when her hemline rises.

Her jewellery tends to be simple, particular favourites being strings of pearls and a beautiful antique gold necklace and earrings set. The latter was made by William Waterhouse, a Dublin jeweller and ancestor of Nick Robinson, and was a special gift to her from her husband's family for her inauguration. She has been seen wearing a hat only once, at the Budweiser Derby in June 1991 and will, it is predicted, never wear one again.

She has been photographed by some of the world's top photographers — Lord Snowdon, Jane Bown, Sebastiao Salgado, Gil Galvin and David Levenson but dislikes posing for photographs. Explaining this to the London *Observer*, she drew an analogy with the old American Indian belief that being photographed was like stealing a bit of your soul.

W ith the President of Pakistan, Ms Benazir Bhutto. President Robinson is wearing an embroidered jacket and skirt by Louise Kennedy.

■ A black and white spotted dress by Pat Crowley worn with matching shoes.

THE

PRESIDENTIAL CAR

Made in 1948, the Rolls Royce Silver Wraith was bought by the Department of Defence in 1949 for the official use of President Seán T. Ó Ceallaigh. Registered ZJ 5000, it has clocked up some 83,000 miles during its many years in service. It has been used by previous Presidents — de Valera, Childers, O'Dalaigh and Hillery — and has carried such dignitaries as President John F. Kennedy, Cardinal Cushing of Boston and Princess Grace of Monaco. It is looked after by the Barrack Master of the Garda Síochána at Garda Headquarters in the Phoenix Park. In 1978 the Rolls Royce Company supervised restoration work on the car and it is now used only on ceremonial occasions.

The Fifth Province

December 1991 President Robinson lighting a candle at Kilmainham Gaol in Dublin during a re-dedication ceremony to mark the 30th anniversary of Amnesty International.

President Robinson told a US interviewer that her office allowed her to think laterally and to do the unexpected. Instinctively recognising the power and potency of symbols, she has shaped a new and imaginative role for the highest office in the land and drawn moral authority from her position as head of state and guardian of its Constitution. A forthright, active and highly visible representative of her state, both at home and overseas, she personifies not only Ireland's strengths, but also, its contradictions.

Being prevented by her office from direct comment on policy matters, she has responded by drawing inspiration from Irish poets, international writers and political thinkers to communicate her ideas while avoiding political minefields. Her speeches and discourses therefore have a philosophical and occasionally a poetic tone. She spoke at Harvard, for instance, about the fragility of the words we speak 'compared to the meanings we want to convey'. Her challenge, as a figurehead of Ireland, is to find a language to express the values she supports, to make use of codes and symbols instead of the more familiar sharpened instruments of the law or politics. Her election in itself was hailed as a signal of change in Irish life, of a new national self-confidence and awareness.

By transforming what has been perceived as a largely ceremonial job, by giving it greater meaning and impetus and by extending the boundaries of the presidential role within the confines of the Constitution, Mary Robinson has changed the face of the presidency forever.

When she visits a small town in Leitrim in the west of Ireland, it is the centre visiting the periphery; when she addresses the UN in New York, it is a small nation addressing the world. In this way she represents the big issues as well as the small print of people's lives. She has constantly said that she would like to be a symbol of peace and reconciliation, to represent the fifth province of the mind.

May 1993 A smiling President Robinson with Lord Jenkins of Hillhead, Chancellor of Oxford University and Roy Foster, the Carroll Professor of Irish History, leaving the Bodleian Library after she received the degree of Doctor of Civil Law by Diploma. The award, said Lord Jenkins presenting her with her scroll, was in recognition of her wisdom and humanity.

■ May 1992 President Robinson receiving an honorary Doctorate of Laws from M. Vivant, Dean of Montpellier University in France which houses Europe's oldest

medical faculty dating from the 12th century. Three deans of the faculty detailed the President's career and praised her work for human

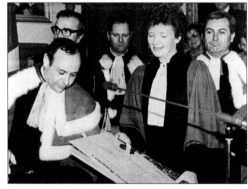

rights. *Le Monde* commented that 'the former feminist lawyer now uses symbols — in the case of the abortion debate as well as Northern Ireland — yet she is herself a symbol of confidence for all Irish women, north and south.'

July 1992 President Robinson on a three-day visit to Scotland, kneels to receive an honorary Doctorate of Laws degree from Sir Kenneth Dover, Chancellor of St Andrews University. St Andrews is Scotland's oldest university and was the first in these islands to admit women as scholars a century ago. President Robinson said that she regarded the honour 'as a symbol of the close and established ties between our two peoples and lands', and in the context of the women's centenary she accepted it with special joy on behalf of 'mná na hÉireann', the women of Ireland.

July 1991 President Robinson lays a wreath at a plaque in the grounds of the Royal Hospital Kilmainham, Dublin, during the National Day of Commemoration ceremonies. Also in attendance were An Taoiseach Mr Charles J. Haughey, representatives of church and state, and members of the public.

October 1991 With Charles Haughey, outgoing Taoiseach, at Áras an Uachtaráin for the first Council of State meeting called by the President since her inauguration. The meeting was called to advise her on the constitutionality of the Fisheries (Amendment) Bill 1990 which was later signed into law.

■ December 1993 President Robinson being greeted by the Very Reverend Maurice Stewart, Dean of St Patrick's when she arrived at the Cathedral for an ecumenical service for peace and reconciliation.

■ November 1993 President Robinson with Prince Karim Aga Khan during a degree ceremony at the University of Wales in Cardiff. Both were awarded honorary degrees by the Prince of Wales.

February 1991 President Robinson planting a tree at Áras an Uachtaráin to launch National Tree Week. Also in the picture are John McCullen (left), president of the Tree Council of Ireland, and Charles Moran (right), head gardener at the Áras. The tree planted replaced one damaged in recent storms.

■ January 1991 Dr T. K. Whitaker, Chancellor of the National University of Ireland, presents President Robinson with an honorary degree of Doctor of Laws at a ceremony in Dublin Castle.

J anuary 1993 President Robinson after lighting a beacon in Dublin's Phoenix Park on New Year's Eve to mark the opening of the single European market.

■ January 1993 An Taoiseach Albert Reynolds receives his seal as head of the Government from President Robinson at Áras an Uachtaráin. A year later she said that relations with the Taoiseach were 'very good' and that 'a lot of trust has been built up on both sides.' The Taoiseach and the President have regular meetings at Áras an Uachtaráin.

February 1991 President Robinson receiving the Freedom of the City of Cork, the fourth president of the state and the first woman to receive the honour. With her is the Lord Mayor of Cork, Mr Frank Nash.

December 1993 President Robinson with members of the Council of State at Áras an Uachtaráin. The Council of State comprises a committee of senior figures who offer advice to the President, when exercising some of her discretionary powers. Five women were appointed to this council on 20 February 1991 reflecting the President's interest in women's affairs. Front left to right: Donal Toolan, founder member of Forum for People with Disabilities; Ceann Comhairle, Seán Treacy TD; An Tánaiste, Dick Spring TD; An Taoiseach, Albert Reynolds TD; President Robinson; Chief Justice, Tom Finlay; President of the High Court, Mr Justice Liam Hamilton; Cathaoirleach of the Senate, Seán Fallon. Back left to right: Quentin Oliver, Director of Northern Ireland Council for Voluntary Action; Monica Barnes, former Fine Gael TD; Patricia O'Donovan, barrister and assistant general secretary of ICTU; Rosemarie Smith, national chairwoman of the Farm Family Committee of the IFA and member of the Council for the Status of Women; Dr Patrick Hillery, former President of Ireland; Attorney General Harry Whelehan; former Chief Justice Tom O'Higgins; Dr T. K. Whitaker, former senator and secretary of the Department of Finance. Not in the photograph is Emer Colleran, Professor of Microbiology at UCG and national chairwoman of An Taisce.

ACKNOWLEDGMENTS

The author would like to acknowledge the generous assistance of the staff of *The Irish Times* library, particularly John Gibson and Tony Lennon, and the *Cork Examiner* and *Sunday Tribune* libraries.

Associated Press (pp 42, 52, 63, 68, 78, 84, 85, 86)

Barry's Photographic Services (pp 33, 120)

John Burke (p 99)

Herma Boyle (p 97)

John Carlos/*The Sunday Tribune* (pp 8, 12, 24, 34, 45, 72, 117)

Cork Examiner (pp 23, 25, 29, 30, 31, 35, 61, 78, 94, 95, 96, 97, 102, 104)

Lesley Doyle (p 52)

Frank Fennell Photography (pp 79)

Tony Gavan (pp 67, 108)

Conor Horgan (p 15)

Hulton/Reuters (pp 62, 63, 65, 77, 82, 103, 117)

The Irish World (p 107)

INOU (p 22)

Inpho Sports Photography (pp 8, 38, 64)

Irish Press (pp 21, 22, 27, 28, 29, 33, 46, 53, 56, 57, 61, 64, 76, 93, 117, 119)

The Irish Times (pp v, 10, 14, 18, 20, 24, 34, 46, 50, 76, 77, 81, 90, 93, 96, 97, 112, 118, 119)

Lucy Johnson (p 47)

Katz Pictures (pp 16, 36)

Lensmen (pp 39, 62, 116, 118, 121)

MacInnes Photography (p 27)

Emmet McCarthy, Clonakilty (p 25)

Maxwell's Photo Agency (pp 10, 26, 38, 47, 68, 98)

National Gallery of Ireland (p 98)

National Park Service: Ellis Island Immigration Museum (p 106)

Pacemaker Press (p 53)

Photocall (pp 43, 58, 60, 65, 66, 67, 92, 108, 110, 111)

Press 22 (pp 80)

Press Association (pp 54, 55, 56, 67, 74, 75, 79, 86, 104, 105, 114, 115)

Reuters/Bettmann (pp 61, 75, 76, 107)

Chris Robson (p 21)

Ray Ryan/*Tuam Herald* (pp 40, 42)

Joe Shaughnessy/*Connacht Tribune* (p 35)

Derek Speirs/Report (pp 20, 26, 28, 32, 44, 54, 110)

Sportsfile (pp 88, 90, 91, 94)

The Star (pp 5, 6, 9, 11, 12, 13, 14, 15, 43)

Ellen Stork Elmendorp (p 69)

The White House (p 69)